GENE KRU[PA]

DRUM METHOD

INTRODUCTION

Gene Krupa is credited with bringing the drum set "to the front of the band." As a soloist and showman, he brought attention to the instrument that paved the way for its expanded and, in fact, predominant role in contemporary music.

Always striving to improve his art, Gene studied the instrument, as well as rhythms of other cultures. In fact, in 1938 he authored a basic drum method which combined individual snare drum techniques with basic drum set applications. That original method comprises the first section of this book. It is a historic look at snare drum and drum set techniques, but also shows how little the basics have changed over the years. The cymbals may have gotten larger, but the content of the method is as valid as it was when first published.

The second section of this publication is totally new. It contains exact transcriptions of Gene's performances as they appear on the DCI video "Jazz Legend" (VH129). These excellent transcriptions by Howard Fields, with commentary by Jim Chapin, show how Gene put together his ideas in actual performance.

The two sections of this historic publication combine the teaching basics and performance practices of the one man who more than anyone else changed the position of the drum set in the musical world.

It has been my pleasure to be part of this project.

Sandy Feldstein

Sandy Feldstein
Publisher

BIOGRAPHICAL NOTE

The most colorful and dynamic personality of "Swingdom" is unquestionably Gene Krupa, the titanic genius of rhythmic drumming. But this creator of a seventh heaven of musical frenzy is more than an entertaining showman; he is acknowledged to be, by drummers and musicians themselves, the foremost living exponent of the art of rudimental and creative drumming.

Gene Krupa was born in Chicago in 1909, and this was especially fortunate for him because Chicago was destined to be the center of the greatest advance of swing music during the years 1924-1930. Those were the years when Fletcher Henderson's orchestra, Louis Armstrong, Frank Teschmacher, Joe Sullivan, Bix Beiderbecke, Bud Freeman, "Baby" Dodds, Pee Wee Russell, Zutie Singleton, Dave Tough, George Whettling, "Wingy" Manone and other great musicians of the Chicago style of jazz music were reaching their greatest heights. Gene listened to these artists, lived with them, played with them, and made many of the recordings that today are rare collectors' items.

Krupa was not satisfied with merely the spontaneous enthusiasm of rhythmic drumming. He felt that there must be an intellectual side to his instrument as with any other, and so he took up the study of rudiments from Sanford E. Moeller, then recognized as the finest teacher in New York. As the result of this study, plus his inherent creative powers, he evolved a style of drumming which has done more for drummers than anything in the history of music. From Vishnudrass Shirali, who plays on 12 drums for Uday Shan-Kar, the Hindu dancer, Gene learned many things about contrapuntal rhythmic combinations. Another great inspiration to his art were the Belgian Congo records made by the Denis-Roosevelt expedition to Africa in 1935.

To return to Krupa's life. When he was thirteen he sat in with his first band, The Frivolians, who were playing at Wisconsin Beach, Wisconsin. Later he was to play with the more famous bands of Red Nichols, Irving Aaronson, Russ Columbo, Mal Hallett and Buddy Rogers.

Then in the year 1935 came the historic meeting with Benny Goodman. Benny gave Gene a featured role in his orchestra, and together with the rise of swing, the stars of Goodman and Krupa began to rise in the firmament. In 1938 came the news of the formation of a band conducted by Gene Krupa himself.

Gene Krupa has made his mark in American jazz as an original and amazingly versatile drummer, and now he makes his debut as an author with this authentic volume on the art of Drumming.

SNARE DRUM, BY VIRTUE OF ITS IMPORTANCE, WILL BE STUDIED FIRST

Practice Pad

Most beginners and many drummers depend upon the drum, instead of themselves, to do the work. It is for this reason that a practice pad is recommended to the student.

Position and form are the first requisites of rudimental drumming. From the correct motions of the hands and arms comes proper muscular development. A snare drum is not conducive to adequate control of the muscles because the sound of the snares influences the beginner by leading him away from the development of a good foundation.

It is not difficult to beat a drum, but picking the beats off the drum at different tempos and with varying shades of volume is an entirely different matter.

The above picture shows the practice pad recommended for your study periods. It is the "table model", which has the advantage of mobility. It can be carried easily from place to place, and with the rubber shock absorbers does not transmit its vibrations to the object it is placed upon.

The pad used in the pictures which illustrate positions is the "stand model", which permits the drummer to sit while playing and to use his feet. It is especially recommended to advanced students.

4

STICKS

Too much cannot be said about the importance of selecting appropriate pairs of drum sticks. For all-around work, hickory has been found to be the most satisfactory wood. The selection of a model must rest with the individual, but it is suggested that he select a stick with a medium taper, as illustrated.

The important things to look for when selecting a pair of sticks are tone, weight and straightness. Each stick has a definite vibration point, depending upon the density and grain of the wood, and it is most important to match the tone of each stick when selecting a pair. This can be done by holding the stick loosely in the right hand and tapping the practice pad. Always test each stick with the same hand. After finding several sticks with identical tones, test them for weight on postal scales. They should weigh exactly the same. Next, roll them along a smooth surface to be sure of their straightness because a warped stick can cause the beginner no end of trouble.

HOLDING THE STICKS

The playing of a snare drum employs the use of sticks, fingers, wrists, elbows and shoulders. At this point it might be well to remind the student that although the sticks are held firmly in the hand, there is never to be any muscular rigidity. Always try to be as relaxed as possible.

THESE TWO PICTURES SHOW THE CORRECT AXIS AND DEVELOPMENT OF HAND TURNING

This picture shows the stick being held in the crotch between the thumb and the area just behind the knuckle bone of the first finger. The distance from the butt of the stick to the point of contact with the hand is about $\frac{1}{3}$ the length of the stick. By taking the position indicated here (notice that the elbow is out, away from the body), you are ready to make a tap.

←

The tip of the stick should be thrown at the pad with an inward turn of the hand and forearm. When the stick strikes the pad, the resiliency of the rubber will cause the tap to bounce back in ascent in the same direction from which it descended.

→

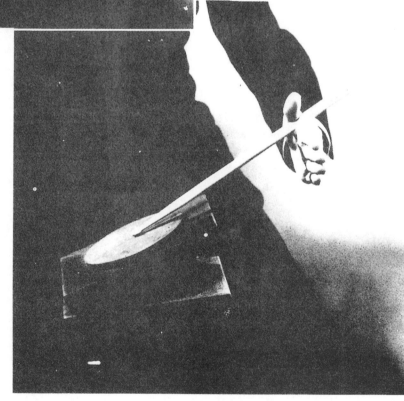

The important part of the exercise on page 5 is the ability to reverse the hand and forearm motion by helping the stick in its movement back, up off the pad. The rebound alone is not powerful enough to swing the tip back to its original position; there must be a quick twist of the hand and forearm to help throw it back. As the stick comes back toward its starting point, the hand and forearm should act as a brake; arresting the backward motion and bringing the stick to a point of muscular resistance similar to the resiliency of the pad. From this point, in an almost continuous motion, the tip is thrown back at the pad, repeating again the entire procedure. This is known as picking beats off the drum. It may seem difficult at first, but a few half-hour practice periods should enable the student to make sharp, clean taps, one for each hand motion. Be sure to press the thumb firmly against the stick to keep it from flopping around. Remember! the tone and volume depend upon the proper execution of the tap, rather than on the mere strength of the blow. After this exercise has been fully mastered, we can proceed to the use of the fingers.

The following pictures show, as clearly as possible, the correct development of the complete finger positions for the left hand. The preliminary stages can best be understood by holding a baseball in the hand, just as a left-handed pitcher would do before throwing a curved ball. (Picture No. 1).

 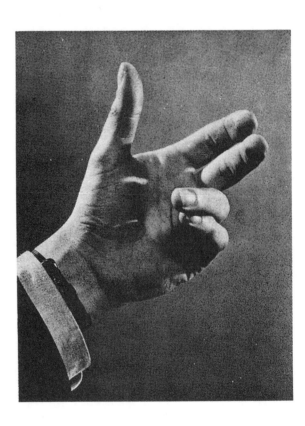

Remove the ball, without disturbing the position of the fingers more than is necessary, and you get a perfect hand position to receive the stick. (Picture No. 2).

Place the stick deep in the crotch and press against it with the thumb, then let the stick rest on the third finger between the first and second joints.

By bringing the first finger over and upon the stick, we have the complete method for holding the left stick. Notice that the second finger is relaxed and acts merely as a guard.

Now, when the stick is thrown at the pad, the third and fourth fingers (which remain together) move down with the turning of the hand to allow the stick full freedom of its axis as it strikes the pad.

The first finger, however, always maintains contact with the stick, the amount of pressure exerted being determined by the volume and number of rebound taps desired.

When the stick comes back, up off the pad, the third and fourth fingers return to their position by the turning motion of the hand and forearm, and help hasten this upward movement. It can readily be seen now that the first finger, and the third and fourth fingers (as a unit) are very important levers, and great care should be exercised while practicing to obtain their correct usage. They are just as important as the correct hand turning, especially when playing soft, delicate passages.

By doing single taps a half-hour daily, the student should soon be ready to progress to the right hand. Make certain however, that you have fully mastered the left hand before proceeding to the right. To be a finished drummer you must be ambidextrous, and with constant practice it is not at all difficult.

Your left hand is the weaker of the two, and does not respond to your brain commands as readily as does your right. This deficiency is merely the result of normal neglect of the left in favor of the right.

The author has found it very helpful to try to do as many things with the left hand as is usually done with the right. Opening doors (the ones with door-knobs being an ideal hand turning exercise), lacing your shoes, carrying parcels, tieing your necktie, buttoning your shirt, feeding yourself at the table, and writing, have been found to be excellent exercises for the left hand.

There are three separate "holds" for the right stick, depending upon the work required of it. The best method to start with is the rudimental foundation from which the others branch.

The stick is held between the inside of the thumb and the first joint of the index finger, as shown in Picture No. 1. Then the remaining fingers are closed lightly around the stick, as in Picture No. 2. Later these fingers are used as control levers, similar to the left-hand fingers. For the present we shall develop the wrist and forearm motion in order to establish good control of the tap.

By taking the position of Picture No. 1 (notice that the right elbow is also out, away from the body) and by turning the forearm (without changing the location of the hand) we get as a result the position in Picture No. 2. By throwing the tip of the stick at the pad, with an inward turn of the forearm and hand, we find ourselves in the position of Picture No. 1 again. As with the left hand, the important part of this exercise is getting the stick back, up off the pad again after producing a sharp, clean tap.

By diligent practice, and a development of the ability to sense at just which point of the hand-turning the tip of the stick strikes the pad; you can also learn to pick the beats off the pad with the right hand and complete the exercise. At first, you may have considerabe trouble due to the stiffness of your wrist. As with the left hand, a few half-hour practice periods should help you master the up-turn. Then you can proceed to use both hands and start the work of two-handed drumming. Everything up to this point is labor of a disheartening sort, but you must go through with it. Remember that most drummers spend years developing themselves to a point of enjoyable proficiency, and you can benefit by that experience if you carefully follow the examples set down in this book. Be careful not to proceed faster than your technique will allow. Everything is pyramided upon preceding lessons. Keep out of bad habits by learning each lesson fully, before going to the next.

After you have fully mastered the correct form for making taps with each hand, we will start using both sticks.

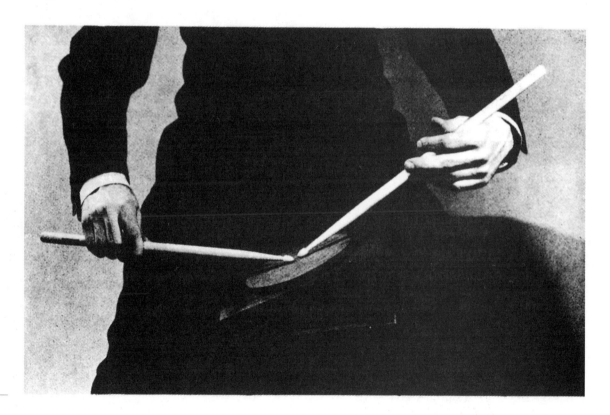

Take position behind pad, as illustrated, with both sticks resting on the pad. Be especially careful to notice the position of the arms and elbows; imagine that you are playing around a barrel. Keep the elbows out so as to permit full freedom of the arms. The power which you need in drumming comes from having your arms out; you really do drum from your shoulders.

HAND TURNING EXERCISE — NO ARM MOTION

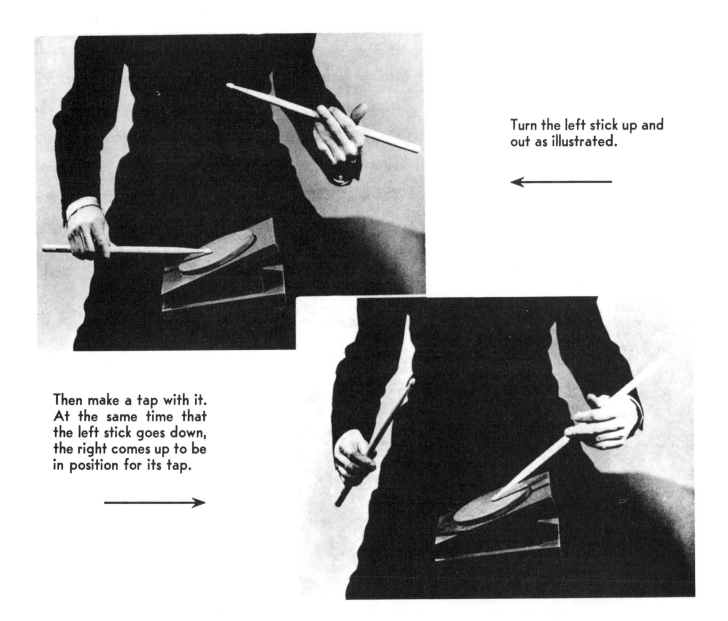

Turn the left stick up and out as illustrated.

←

Then make a tap with it. At the same time that the left stick goes down, the right comes up to be in position for its tap.

→

This movement is known among drummers as "Idle Hand High". It means simply that we wish to utilize all the available time possible by having the idle hand get into position to do its work, while the active hand is working. THIS IS ABSOLUTELY ONE OF THE MOST IMPORTANT POINTS OF RUDIMENTAL DRUMMING. Spend a lot of time on it until you have completely mastered the idea; it must become sub-conscious. This will help develop your speed as much as any form of exercises known.

The student should now acquire a metronome, which is a musical clock for beating time. The pendulum has a movable weight adjustment for varying the tempo. Some models have a bell which rings on the first beat of each measure. The drummer, more than any other musician, is supposed to keep perfect time, and the use of a metronome is highly recommended to help establish that confidence and accuracy.

Now make a tap with the right stick, at the same time bringing the left stick up to be in position. Start this exercise slowly and hold a steady tempo. When you are sure that your form is correct, and that you can keep time easily, take the exercise a little faster, being sure you can execute with relaxation at one tempo before proceeding to the next.

After having mastered single, alternate strokes, proceed to double strokes. Remember "Idle Hand High" (right goes up on first beat of left, and left goes up on first beat of right).

Take this exercise slowly and keep time with the metronome at a tempo of 110; one tap for each tick. Try to move the tempo up one notch each day until a tempo of 180 is reached.

Then proceed to do three taps with each hand.

Then go to four taps with each hand.

The rules which govern double strokes are applicable to three and four. A good way to develop your hand-turning speed is never to go faster with one, two, or three taps than you can with four.

———

Written music is comprised of notes, rests, accents and measures, and other terms used to convey the composer's or the arranger's ideas to the performer. It is not our idea to include a text on the rudiments of music, but a knowledge of the essentials is necessary and is therefore given here.

RUDIMENTS OF MUSIC

The characters which designate the duration of rhythmical sounds are called notes, and are formed thus o 𝅝 𝅗𝅥 𝅘𝅥 𝅘𝅥𝅮 𝅘𝅥𝅯

The position of the notes in the staff indicate which drum: Snare, Bass or Tom-Tom is to be used. Drum music is usually indicated by the Bass Clef sign, but this in no way affects the names of the notes except for Tympani.

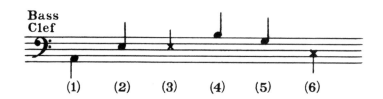

(1) Bass Drum

(2) Snare Drum

(3) Cymbals, and Hi - Hat
when played with sticks

(4) Small (high pitched) Tom-Tom

(5) Large (low pitched) Tom-Tom

(6) Foot Cymbals (Hi - Hat)

MEASURES (BARS) AND SIGNS

The notes are divided into measures (bars) by single or double lines across the staff. One line ≡ is placed after each unit of time— that unit being decided by the time marked at the beginning of each composition. At the end of a composition, or to separate the various sections, double bar lines ≡ are drawn across the staff.

Two dots placed at the double bar lines mean that the section between the two similarly marked double bar lines is to be repeated. If there are no preceeding double bar lines, repeat from the beginning of the composition.

𝄋 Stands for Segno (usually called the sign). It is placed over double bar lines to indicate the beginning of a phrase to be repeated.

Dal Segno (D. S.) means to repeat from the sign.

⌢ The Hold. It is used to sustain a note at the performer's or conductor's pleasure. It often occurs at the end of a composition.

// means sharp stop.

⊕ Is used to mark the beginning of the Coda.

D.S. AL ⌢ means to go back to the sign and play to ⌢

D.S. AL ⊕ means to go back to the sign and play to ⊕ then jump to the Coda.

⌒ The Tie. When placed between two notes it means they are to be played as one.

♩ A dot placed above a note means that the note is to be played short and crisp.

♩ The wedge-like mark indicates an accent, meaning that the note is to be attacked sharply, producing more spirit and volume.

♩. A dot placed after a note increases its value by one-half.

𝄈 means to repeat the preceding bar.

𝄈² When placed across the bar line, with a 2 over it, means to repeat the preceding 2 bars. When a movement is repeated and the last bar (or few bars) changes its character, it is written thus:

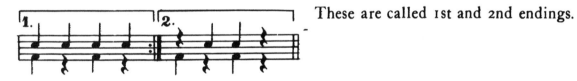 These are called 1st and 2nd endings.

Fp means: Forte-piano, loud and immediately soft again.

Cresc. or ⟨ means: Crescendo, increasing the volume.

Dim. or ⟩ " Decrescendo or diminuendo, diminishing the volume.

⟨⟩ " To begin softly, increase the sound to its loudest and diminish to volume of commencement.

DYNAMICS

P means: Piano, soft.

MP " Mezzopiano — moderately soft.

PP " Pianissimo, very soft.

MF " Mezzoforte — moderately loud.

F " Forte, loud.

FF " Fortissimo — very loud.

sFz " Sforzando — loud, sharply accented.

TEMPO MARKS

Presto — Fast.

Allegro — Quick, lively, vivacious.

Moderato — Moderately.

Andante — A movement in moderate time.

Adagio — Slow and sustained.

Larghetto — Not quite as slow as Largo.

Largo — A very slow and stately movement.

Più — More.

Molto — Much; very much.

Poco — Little.

RELATIVE VALUE OF NOTES AND RESTS

A rest indicates temporary silence. Each note has its rest equal to its value.

Notes   *Rests*

𝗈   Whole Note   ▬   Whole Rest

♩   Half Note   ▬   Half Rest

♩   Quarter Note   ↯   Quarter Rest

♪   Eighth Note   ↱   Eighth Rest

♬   Sixteenth Note   ↱   Sixteenth Rest

♬   Thirty-second Note   ↱   Thirty-second Rest

♬   Sixty-fourth Note   ↱   Sixty-fourth Rest

Comparative Table of the Relative Value of Notes

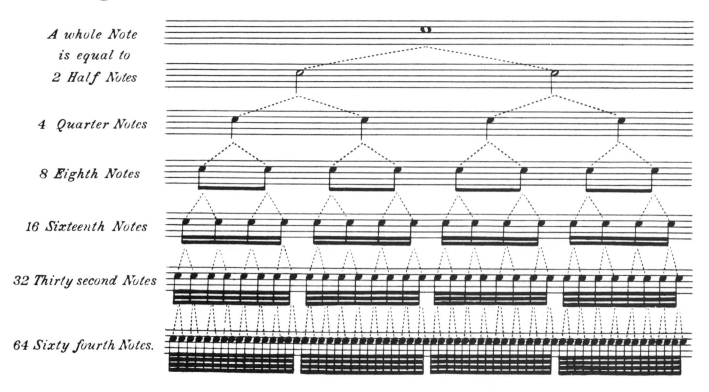

A whole Note is equal to 2 Half Notes

4 Quarter Notes

8 Eighth Notes

16 Sixteenth Notes

32 Thirty second Notes

64 Sixty fourth Notes.

Because drum music requires a great many notes, a set of abbreviations has been adopted which enables the drummer to read with greater ease and speed. These abbreviations also condense a drum score, from what might easily be a small book, to a single sheet of manuscript. This is most evident when music employing a great many rolls is used.

Groups of 8th, 16th and 32nd notes are usually written in combinations, thus:

or abbreviated, thus:

Each of the above abbreviations represents the value of one quarter note.

TRIPLETS AND ARTIFICIAL NOTE GROUPS

Since our system of musical notation lacks characters to represent *third, fifth, sixth and seventh notes* it is necessary for us to group half, quarter, eighth and sixteenth notes into artificial groups and designate their value by placing a number over them.

A Triplet is a group of three notes with the figure above it:

One of the simplest ways to learn to count and play triplets is to start with ¾ time. As you learn to execute them faster say the word "merrily" while playing, to help space the time.

The cross rhythm of 3 against 2 is one of the most seductive known, and a great deal of time can be profitably spent upon the mastery of the following triplet exercises to insure their correct application.

Other artificial groups are:

The time in which a composition is to be played is denoted by numbers placed at the beginning of a composition, or if the time changes, at the beginning of each section of the composition.

The two numbers indicate the value of the notes and the number per measure. A safe and simple rule to follow is to remember that the number above indicates the number of beats or rests per measure, and the number below gives value of the notes:

As can be seen in the above example, there do not have to be four quarter notes, but there must be notes (or rests) that equal 4 quarters.

TABLE OF TIME

*Written as 4/4, but counted in 2

There are other time signatures in use, governed by the same principles shown in the above examples.

It is absolutely imperative that the student be able to count time, and the following exercise should be fully mastered before progressing to the Rolls. A Metronome is indispensible for this exercise.

After doing this exercise several times start with the right stick. Count aloud while practicing and always beat the foot on its first beat of each measure to help keep time.

READING EXERCISES

I.

16th NOTE EXERCISES
VII

EXERCISES WITH DOTTED NOTES

EXERCISES WITH TIES

EXERCISES WITH TRIPLETS

The Upstroke is a time saving motion. It is used for the purpose of getting the hand high (while that hand is making a tap) so as to be in position for making an accented beat or Downstroke.

It is executed by raising the butt of the stick while making a tap with the tip. The following pictures illustrate the correct motions necessary for the proper execution of the Upstroke.

From position number one (picture on left) move the elbow out and up until position number two is reached (picture on right).

Follow the same procedure with the right hand as you did with the left. These pictures can be interpreted better by practicing in front of a large mirror. It is important that you understand these movements clearly because arm motions are now used along with hand turning.

To make an Upstroke we first make a tap, but at the precise instant that the tip of the stick touches the pad move the elbow out and up with a relaxed, graceful, circular movement. Be very careful not to disturb the quality of the tap with any jerky, hurried motions; you have plenty of time in which to raise the butt of the stick. KEEP YOURSELF RELAXED. One bad habit that most students seem to fall into while studying the Upstroke is to turn the butt of the stick too far inward. This can easily be avoided by remembering that the tip of the stick always remains directly above the point of the pad it touched for the tap; it never goes outside the pad.

The following exercises are given to help the student develop the proper execution of the Upstroke.

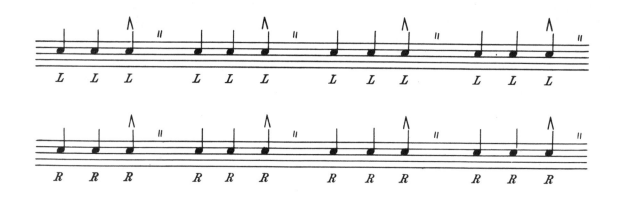

Say to yourself while playing, "tap tap up", then stop, resume your original tap position, and repeat the exercise. It is absolutely impossible to play a series of Upstrokes in succession; the Upstroke is a preparatory motion for the Downstroke which follows. However, we must first learn to make the correct Upstroke. Practice this with both hands until it becomes easy and relaxed, but be sure to return to the tap position after each Upstroke. Be very careful not to disturb the tone and volume of the tap; the Upstroke should sound exactly the same as the preceding taps.

DOWNSTROKE

Without a Downstroke there would be no use for an Upstroke, and without an Upstroke there could be no Downstroke. The Downstroke is a continuation of the Upstroke. They are not two separate rudiments, but are explained that way so as to facilitate the learning of the correct procedure for their execution. The primary function of a Downstroke is to accent the beat. With proper execution, the arm and wrist create a sharply accented tap that adds volume and spirit to what might otherwise become monotonous drumming.

From the completion of an Upstroke (Picture 1) pull the Butt down sharply (Picture 2). When the hand has reached the tap position of Picture 2, a quick snap of the wrist whips the tip of the stick down sharply to make the accented tap and complete the routine. The final movement of the wrist in completing the left Downstroke is very similar to that used in throwing water from the fingers. These successive stages are shown separately, but, when executed, they are rolled into one relaxed round motion.

The complete procedure for a right hand Downstroke is very similar to the left, as illustrated in the above photos. However, the final wrist movement differs in that it resembles the motion used when cracking a whip.

Hereafter an Upstroke will be indicated by a wedge pointing upward and a Downstroke by a wedge pointing downward.

Λ Upstroke   V Downstroke

Naturally this entire routine does take time, but as there are always one or two beats (with the alternate hand) between an Up and a Down stroke, you have sufficient time for proper execution.

THE USE OF UPSTROKE AND DOWNSTROKE

So as not to confuse the student, this exercise starts with a tap and then utilizes the Up and Down strokes throughout. This places the accent on the first beat of the measure. Say to yourself while practicing: "Down Up Tap".

The above exercise changes the placing of the Upstroke to have the Downstroke (accent) come on the 2nd beat. Say to yourself while practicing: "Tap Down Up".

The above exercise changes the placing of the Upstroke to have the Downstroke (accent) come on the 3rd beat. Say to yourself while practicing: "Up Tap Down".

After these three exercises have been learned at a slow tempo, proceed with the same pattern using triplets in ¢ time.

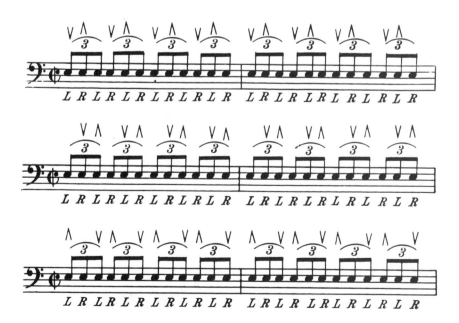

PARADIDDLES

Now that you understand the use of the Up and Downstrokes, we will proceed with their application to the most famous of all rudiments—the Paradiddles.

Paradiddles are used to relieve the monotony of single, alternate taps, and to help the drummer phrase properly the music of the band or orchestra.

Be able to start this exercise with either hand. Say to yourself while practicing: "Down Up Tap Tap". This is known as paradiddle No. 1 with the accent on the first beat.

This is paradiddle No. 2, or as can be seen, it is No. 1 reversed. Say to yourself while practicing: "Tap Tap Down Up". The accent comes on the 3rd beat. Be able to start with either hand.

This is paradiddle No. 3, with the diddle in the middle. Say to yourself while practicing: "Up Tap Tap Down". The accent comes on the 4th beat. Be able to start with either hand.

Now that you have learned the correct hand movements of the three paradiddles, proceed with their application to 8th and 16th note values.

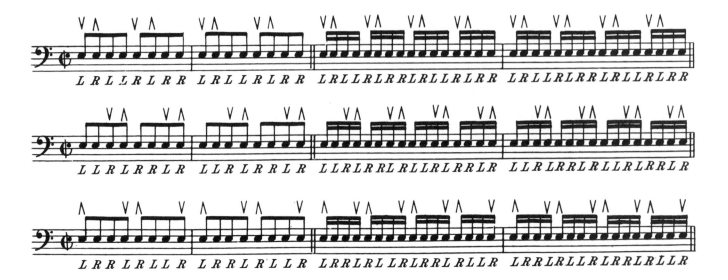

DOUBLE PARADIDDLES

The Double Paradiddles are 3/4 and 6/8 rudiments. They are formed by placing two alternate taps ahead of the three forms of Paradiddles.

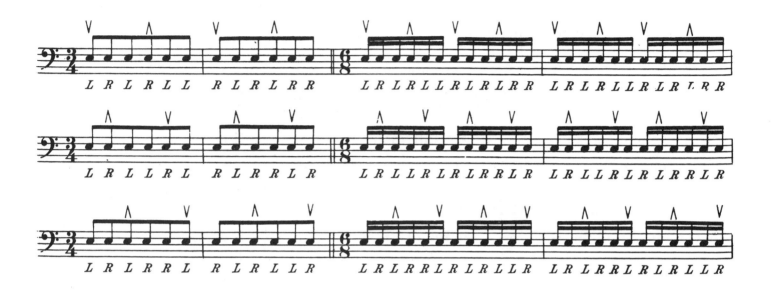

TRIPLE PARADIDDLES

The Triple Paradiddles are formed by placing four alternate taps ahead of anyone of the three forms of Paradiddles.

ROLLS

Because of the percussive character, it is impossible to sustain a note on a Snare drum. Therefore, we take up the study of rolls. A roll is a series of rapid beats in succession which the drummer plays when a sustained note is required of the Snare drum.

Rolls are divided into two classes: The single stroke roll (one tap for each hand movement), and the Daddy Mammy Roll* (two taps for each hand movement).

The single stroke "close rolls" are extremely difficult so we will not hold up the progress of the student by insisting that they be mastered now.

Heretofore the Daddy Mammy has been considered the foundation for all drumming and the author is well aware of the possibility of bringing down upon his head the wrath of the "Elders" for apparently having neglected it until this time. However, experiences with different pupils seem valid enough premises to substantiate his reason for leaving that venerable phase of drumming until this time.

There is no doubt in any drummer's or teacher's mind that such a procedure is an excellent exercise, but because beginners have so much trouble with the gradual closing of the long roll, the following method is substituted.

The Daddy Mammy is the study of taps, two with each stick. In the past, the student was told to start slowly and gradually increase the speed until the taps became so rapid that they closed into a roll. The difficulty always seemed to be in the gradual crossing from the tap to the bounce, so we will take up the study of each separately and then blend them together.

With "Idle Hand High", practice taps, one for each hand motion until a speed of 140 can be maintained comfortably. This exercise is absolutely necessary and must be practiced faithfully until it can be executed with ease.

Start this exercise with either hand and divide your practice evenly between them so as not to became a "one way" player. *Be able to play equally well with either hand!*

* A drummer may and often does roll much closer by using 3 and even 4 rebound taps with each hand movement, but it is much safer for the student to learn to use 1 and 2 at first.

The "bounce", as it is commonly called, is in reality a finger tap. The first beat is made by the wrist and forearm, but the second beat is effected by the fingers' controlling the rebound of the drum while the hand remains down. Instead of following the rebound of the stick, the hand remains low and the control levers (fingers), of which we spoke earlier, force the stick downward for a second beat. Immediately after the second beat, the hand and forearm turn up in the same way as they do after a single tap.

LEFT HAND

Make a tap in the usual manner, but instead of turning the hand up immediately after the tap, keep it low while the first finger presses down on the stick for a second tap before bringing it up. While practicing this beat say to yourself "Daddy Up". Do the exercise again and again until you are sure of two distinct taps; the first with the hand-turning motion, and the second with the control of the rebound by the first finger.

RIGHT HAND

The right hand follows the same procedure as the left hand. The second tap (rebound of the drum) is effected by the second, third and fourth fingers (as a unit) pulling up against the stick. While practicing the right hand say to yourself "Mammy Up".

After each hand has been trained separately, try them together in the following manner:

Play single stroke sixteenth notes at a tempo of 140 on the metronome. Then by superimposing the "Daddy Mammy" (without changing the tempo of the sixteenth note hand movement) you will find yourself making thirty-second notes. In other words you will have gone a long way toward closing the Roll. After you have gone over this exercise several times, you will not have any trouble practicing the "Daddy Mammy" alone.

Next we learn to open the "Daddy Mammy" by gradually slowing down the speed. You will find as you decrease the speed that it will be hard to maintain adequate control of the second rebound-beat or finger tap. When you arrive at this point, make two taps, one for each hand motion, without utilizing the bounce. Then it will be very easy to slow your taps down gradually to a very slow tempo. Do this over and over, until you can cross the "HUMP";* then come out of the fast "Daddy Mammy" to a slow tap tap, gradually, and without any noticeable breaks. After you have mastered this exercise, you should have no trouble in closing the tap tap to a "Daddy Mammy" Roll. It is recommended that you establish perfect control in coming out of the "Daddy Mammy" into the taps before you try to go from the taps into the "Daddy Mammy." With conscientious effort you should be able to gain fairly good control of the opening and closing of the long roll. From now on this is your warm-up exercise; 10 minutes daily before your regular practice session, close and open the "Daddy Mammy".

* The "HUMP" is a term applied to the difficult transition from tap to bounce, and bounce to tap. You should be able to cross this particular point without any noticeable change in the speed and sound of the roll.

ROLL CHART

This chart is for use with rolls that are superimposed upon 16th note single stroke hand motion.

	3 STROKE ROLL				2 HAND MOTIONS		ALTERNATES
♪				....			
	5	"	"	....	3	" "	"
	7	"	"	....	4	" "	BEGINS WITH L
	9	"	"	....	5	" "	ALTERNATES
	11	"	"	....	6	" "	BEGINS WITH L
	13	"	"	....	7	" "	ALTERNATES
	15	"	"	....	8	" "	BEGINS WITH L
	17	"	"	....	9	" "	ALTERNATES

THE RUFF

We take up the study of the Ruff at this point because every Roll ends with it.

Make a "Daddy" with the left and a tap with the right, with the tap following immediately after the "Daddy."

Then make a "Mammy" with the right and have the left come right after the "Mammy."

In this exercise have the "Daddy" and "Mammy" hands turn up after the rebound so as to be high for the accented, single tap, which comes on every other hand.

5 STROKE ROLL

First we get the foundation of 3 hand movements, alternating from hand to hand.

Then by placing two 16th note taps on each of the eighth notes we have an open 5 stroke Roll.

While playing, say "tap up tap tap down". Spend a lot of time on this and you will save yourself a lot of headaches later, because all rolls larger than the 5 stroke end with a 5 stroke.

To get a closed 5 stroke Roll we superimpose the "Daddy Mammy" on the following foundation of 3 hand movements.

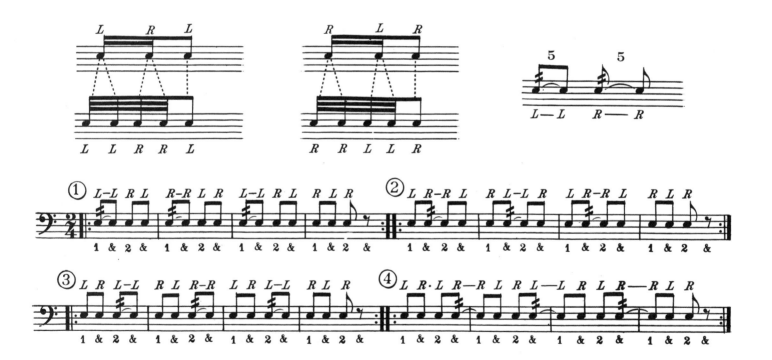

9 STROKE ROLL

To make a 9 stroke Roll superimpose the "Daddy Mammy" on the following foundation of 5 hand movements:

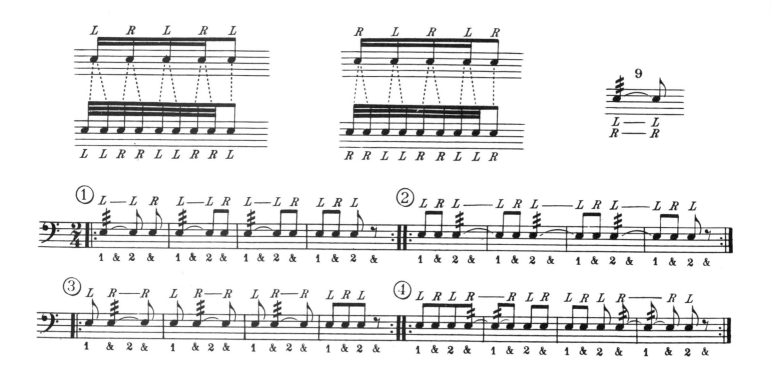

13 STROKE ROLL

To make a 13 stroke Roll superimpose the "Daddy Mammy" on the following foundation of 7 hand movements:

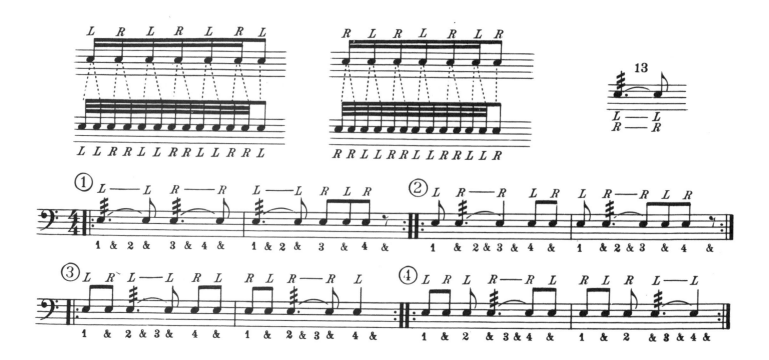

7 STROKE ROLL

4 hand movements always begin with left.* This is the first of a series of rolls that differs from the three just studied in that they end on the off beat, leaving only a 32nd note rest between the end of the roll and the following note.

Foundation or hand movement:

By superimposing the "Daddy Mammy" on this we get:

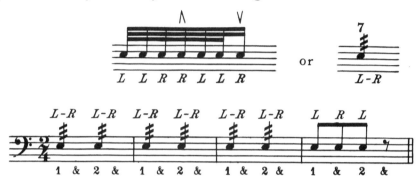

*It is a good idea to be able to play the 7 stroke Roll by starting with either hand, but when they come in series it is always safer to start with the left hand.

11 STROKE ROLL

6 hand movements always begin with left.* Foundation or hand movement:

By superimposing "Daddy Mammy" on this we get:

*Be able to play by starting with either hand. Footnote of 7 stroke Roll applies to this roll also.

8 hand movements always begin with the left.* Foundation or hand movements:

By superimposing "Daddy Mammy" on this we get:

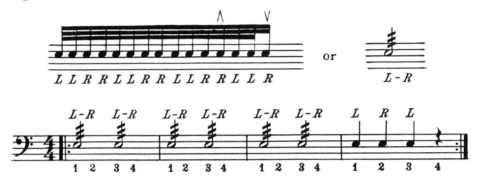

*Be able to play by starting with either hand. Footnote of 7 stroke Roll applies here also.

TRIPLET ROLLS

7 Stroke

By changing the foundation (hand movement) you can change the value of a roll without changing its time of duration.

By substituting a 16th note triplet for the two sixteenth notes of a 5 stroke Roll foundation you get the following foundation:

By superimposing "Daddy Mammy" on this hand movement you get a 7 stroke Roll:

This can be written and played (substituted in place of a 5 stroke Roll and often is.

The number 7 above the 5 stroke Roll indicates that it is to be played as a seven. This is used very frequently, and is more common than the 16th note hand movement 7 stroke.

Its use depends upon the discretion of the performer, but when the tempo is slow it is recommended in place of the straight 5 stroke.

13 Stroke

By changing the hand movement (foundation) of a 9 stroke Roll you get a 13 stroke Roll.

It is written as a 9 (taking the same length of time to execute) but played as a 13.

By substituting 16th note triplets for the four 16th notes of a 9 stroke foundation you get the following:

By superimposing 32nd note "Daddy Mammy" on the above foundation you get a 13 stroke Roll:

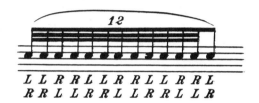

This can be written and played (substituted) in place of a 9 stroke Roll and often is.

The number 13 above the 9 stroke Roll indicates that it is to be played as a 13.

Here, as with the triplet 7, its use depends upon the discretion of the performer.

TRIPLET ROLLS OF LONGER DURATION

Many times a drummer is called upon to use triplet hand movement when rolling, and for rolls that exceed the 7 and 13 stroke the following Key is offered. Because very few arrangers and composers have seen fit to make even a cursory examination of the existing drum rudiments it will be up to the drummer to substitute his own interpretation.

It is hoped that this explanation will be of service to you, and although it has never been written before, it has a decided value in the field of modern drumming.

Hand Motion (Foundation)

By superimposing "Daddy Mammy" on the above, a roll having triplet hand motion is effected.

ROLLS OF EIGHTH NOTE HAND MOVEMENT

Cut time ¢ is written as 4/4 but counted like 2/4. It usually has the pulsation of two beats to the bar much the same as 6/8 time.

This clearly illustrates the need for rolls of 8th note hand movement, because if a drummer tries to put in the value of the written score at the tempo in which these are usually taken, he will become very tired after playing but a few measures.

Short Rolls can usually be played with a triplet hand movement, but the long Rolls should have the 8th note foundation, especially in the 6/8 time.

The following studies are offered to help you form your own interpretation of the printed score:

Here you should use the 5 stroke Roll or the triplet 7, depending upon the tempo.

Although this is actually a 17 stroke Roll, you should use a 9 stroke or triplet 13, depending upon the tempo.

A 5 or triplet 7 stroke Roll can be used. Either is acceptable.

Here the 8th note hand movement 7 stroke is preferable, and in all rolls of larger duration you should use 8th note hand movement because it fits the pulsation of 6/8 marching time.

EVEN NUMBER ROLLS

The following group of rolls are not generally known, but are very effective when used properly. They differ from the other rolls in that they all end with two single taps instead of a ruff.

The simplest way to learn each one is to make the odd number roll of the denomination just below, and then add a single tap with the opposite hand in the time of the hand motion used for the regular rolls.

4 STROKE ROLL

Make a 3 stroke roll and add a single tap.

Played like  3 hand motions, alternates.

6 STROKE ROLL

Make a 5 stroke roll and add a single tap.

Played like 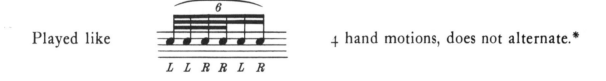 4 hand motions, does not alternate.*

8 STROKE ROLL

Make a 7 stroke roll and add a single tap.

Played like  5 hand motions, alternates.

10 STROKE ROLL

Make a 9 stroke roll and add a single tap.

Played like  6 hand motions, does not alternate.*

* But should be learned both ways.

DRAG PARADIDDLES

The Drag Paradiddle is very similar to the Flamadiddle* except that it employs the use of a Ruff (now called a Drag) instead of a Flam. It is a very difficult rudiment and requires intensive practice.

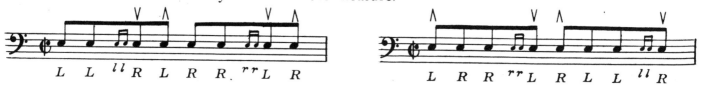

As can be seen, the difficulty lies in getting the Drag between the diddle and the downstroke with the same hand that made the diddle. The two grace notes (drag) are an embellishment and do not detract any time from the measure.

RL RL R R L R
L R R L R L L R

The Drag should be played lightly and cleanly—do not rub the drum, pick them off.

DRAG PARADIDDLE No. 2

RATAMACUES

By rolling the R of the name of this rudiment, you get an excellent idea of how it should sound. The three forms of Ratamacue use the drag beat, triplet and tap. They are easy, swinging rudiments and are very effective when properly used. Notice that the accent comes on the first beat of the triplet.

Single Ratamacue

Double Ratamacue

Triple Ratamacue

* To follow later.

SINGLE AND DOUBLE DRAGS

Drags have always been considered the most difficult of all rudimental beats. The trouble has usually been with their correct application to time rather than their execution, because many students have been able to play drags immediately upon hearing someone execute them correctly. The drags do appear at very unusual places in the measure so we shall try to clear up that point first, and give the student a clear understanding of what he wants to do before he develops any mental hazards.

The above exercise should be played correctly before any drags are attempted. Most students have a habit of playing this measure so that it sounds like a measure of 6/8 and that is where a great deal of trouble arises. There is quite a difference between the two measures. Break them down into 16th notes and you will find the difference easily.

The 16th note of the measure of ₵ is shorter by one-half than the 8th of the 6/8 measure and comes much closer to the following dotted 8th. This gives an entirely different character to the ₵ time.

To play it correctly, practice this exercise:

After making sure of the correct playing of the exercise, practice the following:

bed Tom - bed Tom-bed Tom -bed Tom-bed

While playing, say to yourself "bed Tom, bed Tom, bed Tom, etc." Notice how quickly the word Tom comes after bed, and the pause between Tom and bed (the words must coincide with the correct playing of the notes).

When you are sure of playing this correctly, proceed to the following:

With the opposite hand put the drag (as late as possible after Tom and as quickly as possible before bed) between the dotted 8th and 16th note hand taps, saying meanwhile: "bed Tom-(go t'bed) Tom, (go t'bed) Tom, (go t'bed) Tom, (go t'bed), etc".

Be sure to accent Tom and bed, but the drags should be light, and crisp—no crushing! This is usually written in 2/4 and ¢ time. After you have learned to play the time correctly, you will get a swinging style that will help keep your hands and wrists from tiring.

DOUBLE DRAG

The Double Drag is a 6/8 rudiment and is made by adding a Drag ahead of the Single Drag. The fingering for the Double Drag foundation is:

By adding the Drags we get:

While playing, say to yourself "(go t'bed) (go t'bed Tom), (go t'bed) (go t'bed Tom)". As with the Single Drag the grace notes should be light and crisp—no crushing!

SINGLE STROKE ROLLS
3 Stroke Roll

This rudiment goes from hand to hand. The hand that plays the second tap goes a little higher than the other, to be ready to start the next roll. You will often find this roll written as an embellishment, and when a phrase like this occurs in unison with the orchestra it is better to play it single stroke.

4 STROKE ROLL (RUFF)

This rudiment goes from hand to hand (alternates) because it has a graceful, swinging motion when played that way.

By raising the hand that makes the third tap a little higher than the other, the swing of the rudiment is improved, and greater speed can be attained.

You will sometimes find it written thus:

5 STROKE ROLL (RUFF)

This rudiment goes from hand to hand (alternates). By raising the hand that makes the third tap a little higher than the other, you are in a better position to give the last beat a sharp accent and give the roll a better finish.

As written:

This is also an embellishment and does not detract from the value of the measure.

7 STROKE ROLL

This is a very useful and graceful single stroke Roll that has a great deal of use in modern drumming. It goes from hand to hand (alternates), and because of its rhythmic character is a very important rudiment for dance drumming.

RUFF PARADIDDLES

3 Stroke Ruff Paradiddle

4 Stroke Ruff Paradiddle

Notice that this differs from the 3 stroke by having the same hand that played the diddle start the ruff.

5 Stroke Ruff Paradiddle

COUMPOUND BEATS

PARATRIPLETS

FLAMS

A flam is a regular tap preceded by a grace note. The grace note is lighter than the tap and should come as close as possible to the tap. A correctly made flam should sound like the word "Plum"—the grace note being the "P" and the tap, "lum".

This rudiment alternates.

Be sure to play this rudiment from hand to hand because it is very easy to get into the habit of making all the grace notes with one hand.

To make a correct flam have the right stick about two inches above the pad while the left is about ten inches higher. Now, by turning both hands and attempting to make a tap with both sticks at once you will find yourself making a flam because one stick has less distance to travel and gets there first.

The right, or low hand, goes high to position left had before making the flam, and the high hand, left, stays low in same position right had before the flam. After each flam the sticks are in reversed positions.

Practice the flam very slowly so as to be sure to get correct hand positions. Stop after each flam until you are sure the low hand strikes first, then progress to a series of them, making sure of alternate hand movements.

The flam is used to thicken the beat, and to give it an accented character. Its most effective use is with drum corps and brass band music, where crisp percussion is most valuable.

Flams are also used a great deal when playing on the wood block and rim of the snare and bass drum.

FLAMACUE

This rudiment uses the flam hand movements and therefore should be studied at this time.

The rudiment alternates, and while executing say to yourself, "Flam Down Up Tap Flam". With right hand low make a flam, right goes high and left remains low ; then make a downstroke with right (at same time turn up left tip with hand turning). Now make an upstroke with left (right remains low), then make a tap with right, right remains low for grace note of flam which is the last beat of this rudiment; hands should now be in reversed position, and the entire routine is repeated with the hands in opposite positions.

This is the way the flamacue is written. Notice the accent mark for the downstroke. To get the correct character of this rudiment the downstroke should be accented sharply.

FLAM TAP

This rudiment is made just as the name sounds, "plah-tah plah-tah", etc. It is a very useful and beautiful rudiment, and if executed with relaxed muscles can be closed to a roll.

To execute, simply make a flam, high hand stays low to make the tap and grace note, and then goes high while opposite hand comes down to do the same work in the alternation.

To close this rudiment simply place a grace note ahead of an open "Daddy Mammy" (with the opposite hand), and alternate as illustrated. Start slowly to be sure of correct hand motions, and you will have no trouble when you wish to attain more speed. As you incorporate the bounce of the drum in closing, eliminate the arm motion and use only hand-turning as you did in closing the roll.

This is merely a flam tap in 6/8 time:

Use the arm motion to help get correct swing. It can also be used as follows:

FLAM ACCENT No. I

This is essentially a 6/8 or triplet rudiment and although not usually shown can be played in two ways:

Notice that the grace note hand R does not go up as it did when making alternate flams or flam taps, but *remains low so as to be in position to make the upstroke.*

Left hand makes tap while right is swinging up to be high for alternate flam. The second half of the rudiment is exactly like the first except that the hands are reversed. Say to yourself while practicing "Flam up tap", etc.

As with the others, take this rudiment slowly until you are sure of correct hand motions.

Method No. 2 for fingering a flam accent is shown because it does have a character somewhat different from No. 1, and there are times when its use is to be desired, especially when playing fast.

This method does not reverse while playing, but it should be learned both ways. No upstroke is used in this method; hand turning alone is needed.

To get speed use the "Daddy" or "Mammy" for the two taps and you will find the other hand (that makes grace notes and last beat of the group of three), giving a decided 6/8 beat!

It is suggested that you master the first method before the second, and use your own judgment when to apply either one.

Method No. 3 is also shown because there are times when its use is to be desired over the other two.

Flam Accent No. 1 does not have to be confined to 6/8 and triplet time; it can be used for excellent syncopation as the following exercise shows:

FLAMADIDDLES

These are very old and very difficult rudiments, but very important. They will help develop your technique considerably, but don't expect to acquire any speed with them until after several months of hard practice.

They are simply paradiddles with a grace note (flam) ahead of each downstroke. The form is exactly the same as the first method of playing Flam Accent No. 1, except that you have two taps instead of one following the upstroke. The difficult part of this rudiment is getting the flam in ahead of the first beat with the same hand that played the two taps, or diddle.

Do you understand now why it is so necessary to do the preliminary exercises of 1, 2, 3 and 4 taps with each stick?

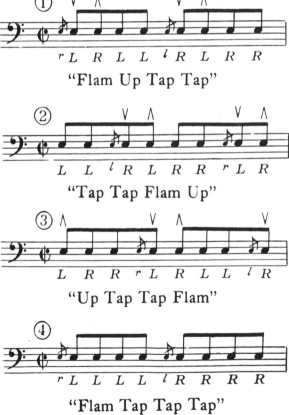

① "Flam Up Tap Tap"

② "Tap Tap Flam Up"

③ "Up Tap Tap Flam"

④ "Flam Tap Tap Tap"

BASS DRUM

The bass drum is extremely important in the modern band and orchestra and a great deal of time should be spent upon exercises to improve the coordination of feet and hands.

Bass drum is played with a pedal which is manipulated by the right foot. The drummer should sit fairly high so as to allow the leg and ankle complete freedom and relaxation. The heel should be the axis of the foot movement. Be very careful not to allow the beater ball to remain against the head after the beat—try to pick the beats off of the drum by getting the foot back to the position from which it started the beat. This will give you a sharp, clean boom and improve your speed a great deal.

Many drummers neglect to practice bass drum as much as their snare because of the disturbance caused by the loud sound of the drum. This can be easily overcome by getting a pedal practice pad which has the advantage of allowing you to use your own pedal. Of course this isn't a bass drum, but you will find it better than allowing your leg muscles to remain idle. It is recommended that you put as much time on your bass drum practice as you do on your snare drum.

EXERCISES FOR BASS DRUM

(By anticipating the accented *ah* you can count this so it will sound as it should be played).
"Jump" the *ah* by anticipating it with sharp attack!

FOOT CYMBALS (HI HAT)

Hi Hat cymbals are played with the left foot. They were originally intended to be used for an after beat (off beat) cymbal effect, and as they are still very useful for that purpose, we will start our study from that point.

SELECTING THE CYMBALS

It is suggested that you select two eleven-inch *Avedis* Zildjian cymbals for your Hi Hat, because you will find them most satisfactory for all around work.

Select two medium thin, low-pitched cymbals, and have the one for use underneath a little heavier and a little lower in pitch—don't use cymbals with a strong fundamental (bell tone) on your Hi Hat. Try to get cymbals that are rich in harmonic overtones—that "splash" instead of ring.

Be very careful not to get them too thin, or they might buckle, and don't get them too thick or they might sound high-pitched and tinny. They should have a level of tonality, when struck with the sticks, that will blend with the brass section.

MOUNTING THE CYMBALS

To mount the cymbals for best results use five soft felt washers, one under the bottom cymbal, two under the top cymbal and two between the wing nut and the top cymbal.

Don't screw the wing nut too tight; keep it at a point of pressure allowing the top cymbal freedom of a wobbly movement, but with no up-and-down play when you depress the pedal. This point will vary and you can always keep the tension right by a simple adjustment of the wing nut. Don't remove your cymbals from the Hi Hat stand because they become "seated" after being used for a time and will work better in their own groove.

FOOT WORK

The foot work is a very important part of good Hi Hat playing and it is suggested that you learn to work your foot alone before trying to combine the Hi Hat with bass drum practice. As stated before, the Hi Hat is essentially an after-beat cymbal that plays on the off beat of the bar. After you have mastered the use of the left foot for opening and closing the Hi Hat let us proceed to the use of both feet.

When the right foot (bass drum) goes down, the left foot (Hi Hat) comes up, and when the left goes down, the right comes up—an alternating foot movement like the single strokes on the snare drum. Don't lift the left foot too high—an inch to an inch-and-a-half opening between the cymbals gives the best results.

After you have practiced this long enough to do it easily at tempo 110 on the metronome, go on to the next exercise.

Here the left foot movements for the Hi Hat remain exactly the same as in the preceding exercise, but the right (bass drum) plays every beat in the bar. Make sure while practicing this exercise that the bass drum and Hi Hat come together simultaneously on beats 2 and 4. When you can do this exercise comfortably at tempo 110 proceed to the next.

In this exercise both feet are played together. It can be played to sound four different ways:

(1) By raising both feet together you can get a "ching" "ching" "ching" sound.

(2) By holding the left foot down just a little longer than the right, you stop the sustained quality of the cymbal tone and get a "chick" "chick" "chick" sound.

(3) By holding the left foot down a little longer on counts 1 and 3 you get a "chick" "ching" "chick" "ching" effect.

(4) By holding the left foot down a little longer on 2 and 4 you get a reverse, or "ching" "chick" "ching" "chick" effect.

To get the "chick" sound you hold the cymbals down a little longer, as explained.

To get the "ching" sound, slap the cymbals together and raise the foot quickly to allow them to sustain their tones.

These beats are quite tricky because you must effect the various sound combinations without disturbing the unison foot work of bass drum and Hi Hat, and *also keep steady time.* Start it slowly and master each exercise before proceeding to the next and you will not have much trouble—just take it slowly!

PLAYING HI HAT WITH STICKS

You must now be "Quadridextrous" (if we may be allowed to coin a word) because you have to use both feet and both hands, each playing different rhythms on different instruments at the same time. Hi Hat is usually played with the right stick, but sometimes both hands are used for making single stroke rolls or various rhythmic figures.

While the feet are playing the above measures the right hand plays the following:

o means that the left foot is up (cymbals are open).

x means that the left foot is down (cymbals are closed).

When this beat is made correctly it will sound:

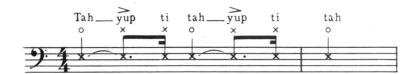

After you are able to play the preceding exercises with ease, incorporate the use of the left hand (playing single, accented taps on the snare drum) as follows:

The left hand plays the notes indicated by the marks in the C space (second from the top) of the staff.

The accent marks are good for right on Hi Hat, left on snare drum (rim shot, if desired), left foot on Hi Hat and right foot on bass drum. This is a very important fundamental beat for dance drumming; keep it "jumping", don't let it drag.

The pictures on the following page illustrate the hand positions in playing this beat.

Recommended for soft playing.

Recommended for loud playing.

4 STROKE RUFF ON HI HAT

This is the next Hi Hat beat (very useful for dance drumming) which we shall study at this time because it employs the use of both hands while the feet are playing beat of Exercise 1 on page 57. The hands play any one of the following:

Or to add a "jump" beat the following:

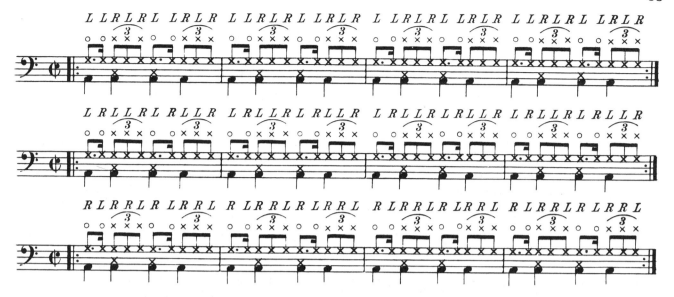

7 STROKE ROLL (SINGLE STROKE) ON HI HAT

After the foregoing has been learned we can proceed to the following:

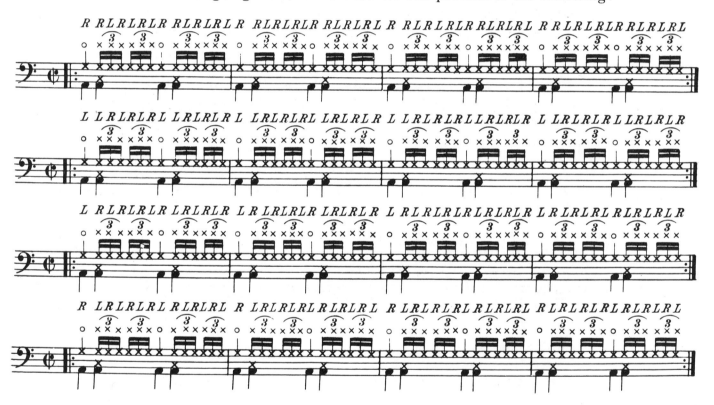

Or, as with the four stroke, to add a "jump" beat as follows:

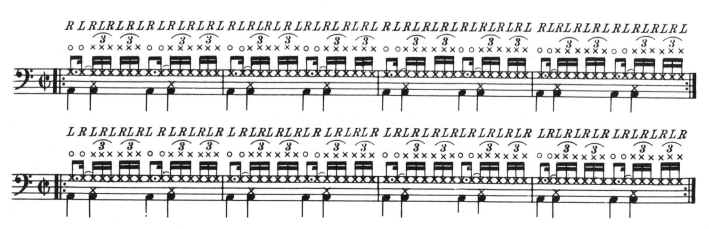

The following three pictures illustrate the different positions that can be used when playing the Hi Hat with both sticks. Each position gives a different tonal effect, and it is your job to use the one which gives the required results.

SOME SYNCOPATED BEATS FOR HI HAT

The following are derivations of what has gone before, and although not difficult, are very effective when used properly:

As will be observed, the second bar may need some explaining: the right hand plays the "jump" beat as indicated, and where the note appears (no stick) only the bass drum, Hi Hat and left stick play the beat. The right hand plays again on the 16th following. The left stick (snare drum) and right foot (bass drum) are playing regular 4/4 rhythm against this anticipated accent.

Instead of the right stick always playing the anticipated beat, it can be done with the left for a rim shot if desired, and creates a very fine rhythmical effect when alternated every two bars—first Hi Hat "jump" beat and then left rim shot "jump" beat, against regular ¢ Hi Hat and bass drum rhythm.

Another fine effect which can be used effectively is the striking of the Hi Hat stand with the left stick about 8 inches below the cymbals. Instead of using the left stick on the snare drum or on Hi Hat, a variety of beats can be worked out by striking the cymbal stand. It gives a high pitched ringing sound of excellent percussive character. Pictures 1 and 2 illustrate the hand positions. Notice in Picture 2 how a fine effect can be obtained by striking the butt of the left stick with the right tip; this gives you four different tonal effects from this one position.

PLAYING WITH HI HAT CLOSED

By keeping the left foot down (cymbals closed) a variety of useful effects can be obtained by resorting to the standard rudiments as played on snare drum.

CYMBALS AND CYMBAL PLAYING

The drummer with a standard dance orchestra should have four cymbals with different tones mounted on stands or bass drum so as to be within easy reach of his right stick.

My cymbals are mounted as illustrated:

Each cymbal has its own tone and response and you learn to play your cymbals by knowing how sharply and with what power to get the required tonal results. Another thing not generally known is that cymbals improve with age. After being beaten for sometime they become more tempered and less stiff. This molecular realignment usually improves the response and tone of a cymbal. However it sometimes has the opposite effect and the cymbal becomes worthless, but as this happens very rarely, the rule is generally for improvement.

The cymbal at my left is a 13-inch *Avedis* Zildjian. It is high pitched and of medium weight. This cymbal is used for stick and brush work, and is mounted so as to be easily accessible to either hand. This cymbal should have a quality of tone that will cut through the orchestra. It is known as a "fast" cymbal because it responds quickly when struck with a stick or brush. It is used before and after phrases, and to reinforce heavy brass figures with unison beats. It is used more than any other cymbal, and therefore great care should be exercised in its selection.

The above picture shows how the cymbal is played with the tip of the stick.

The above picture shows how the stick strikes the cymbal when a full tone is desired. The left hand is used to catch the cymbal to stop the duration of the tone at any desired place.

With the left hand choking the cymbal, as illustrated, many fast combinations of beats can be effected by the use of the tips of both sticks. The left comes up against the bottom of the cymbal and the right strikes it from the top.

The cymbal second from the left is an 8-inch thin Zildjian to be used always open. Just hit it and let it ring because it is rich in harmonics and has no sustaining bell tone. It is used as a "splash" cymbal to give the same effect as a small Chinese cymbal.

The cymbal third from the left is a lower-pitched medium, thick, 14-inch Zildjian, used a great deal for playing with the tip of the right stick.

The cymbal on the extreme right on the stand is a 16-inch, of medium thickness, used to end climaxes, and where great volume is desired. It is also very good for sustained tones to be effected by rolling on it with tympani strokes.

PLAYING SNARE DRUM WITH BRUSHES

The kind of brushes most adaptable to rudimental drummers are the round handled, telescope variety with rubber tubing over the handle. Their weight and size make them comparable to sticks.

It is possible to play, with brushes, practically everything that you do with sticks. The one exception is the closed roll. For the roll a swish effect is substituted. This is made by several different methods:

The following pictures show progressive stages of the first brush rudiment.
First make a tap with the left hand. While making a tap with left, right gets into position (idle hand high). On second beat both brushes strike the drum together (picture at left). Right brush is drawn across the head of the drum with an arm motion that pulls across the body. At the same time the left hand goes up to make tap 3. (Picture at right).

This swish movement of the right hand continues to the third beat at which precise instant it is lifted up with a wrist movement while the left hand makes the third tap. Then, when left makes tap 4, it comes down again.

Brush rolls are written just like snare drum rolls, but are played:

This entire procedure should also be practiced in reverse, because it is played a great deal both ways.

This rudiment can also be played with the left hand alone, leaving the right free to play the Egyptian ("Greeko") cymbal, tom-tom, or any of the other cymbals as desired. To execute, make a tap with left about half way between the rim and center of the drum, then raise the brush and move your arm across to far side of drum for second beat; drag the brush toward you until first tap position is reached and repeat the procedure.

Now, while left is doing the above exercise, right can be doing the following:

By describing clockwise circles with the right brush on the tom-tom, one for each quarter note, a very insinuating rhythm can be developed. Without lifting the right brush from the tom-tom, make small circles on beats 1 and 3, and larger circles on beats 2 and 4. You will have to move faster to get around on beats 2 and 4 and this will cause you to give a little accent or push.

The following pictures illustrate a brush rudiment that sounds much the same as number 1, but as it utilizes all motions for beats, it is an excellent substitute for fast tempos.

The left hand beats single taps while the right produces a swish for each hand turning; away from the body for the second beat, and toward the body for the fourth beat.

All the beats that were explained for Hi Hat playing with sticks can be done with brushes, and are recommended for soft swing.

RIM SHOTS

Many drummers worry about their rim shots because they claim that they miss as often as they hit, especially when playing fast tempos. To gain confidence in making rim shots remember your first lesson, HAND TURNING ONLY, NO ARM MOTION, and IDLE HAND HIGH.

The following pictures illustrate clearly the different methods for making rim shots, and each method produces a different tone. For recording and radio work the cross stick type produces less needle jump and are therefore safer to use for that particular purpose. For fast "cute" rim shots, stay close to the rim, but for masculine, pile driving "zonks", get to the center of the drum.

DANCE ROLL RUDIMENTS

Press Roll (fast tempos).

7 Stroke Roll (medium fast tempos).

9 Stroke Roll (medium tempos).

13 Stroke (triplet) Roll (slow tempos).

Although these rolls are all written the same, they should be played as indicated to give the most solidity to the rhythm section.

Don't tune your drums too tight. Keep them at a tension allowing maximum tone!

The author sincerely believes that the student can gain a great deal of practical knowledge by playing drums with a phonograph, and it is for this reason that the following scores are presented. They may not be exactly as played, but they are close enough to give you a clue as to what is "going on". He sincerely hopes that you will derive as much pleasure from studying them as he had in making them.

Music Key

H.H.	✗		● Ride Cym.		●– Crash Cym.	✱– Splash Cym.	✗ Cowbell
T.T.							
S.D.			✗ rim shot		⊗ stick shot*	⊘ cross stick	
F.T.							
B.D.			✗ B.D. w/left hand				
H.H.	✗						
w/foot							

*In the 1930s, placing the tip of the left stick on the snare skin and then striking it (the left stick) with the right stick, was referred to as a "cross stick." Herein this is called a "stick shot" and in this way will not be confused with the modern day implication of "cross stick" which refers to the left stick being layed across the snare drum with the fat end of the stick striking the rim thereby creating the characteristic wood block sound.

The drum transcriptions herein, while they very accurately reflect the audio portions of the "Gene Krupa: Jazz Legend" video, are at times not totally faithful to what one sees (such as toms being heard while the snare alone is clearly being struck, etc.). The reason for these imperfections may have been that the music on some of the film used, had to be overdubbed after the filming was done. It's entirely possible then that Gene, having to perfectly recreate his drum parts and solos, may have not remembered every last riff, note-for-note. It's difficult to say what exactly went on with archival films of this type but fortunately these instances are at a minimum.

The Big Noise From Winnetka

This first track on the video portrays Gene late in his career (1967). The fills and solos he plays in the tune make use of a few of the various techniques he developed over the course of almost 50 years of drumming. The delightful cowbell lick used in Drum Fill 2, the sparseness of the first few bars of Drum Solo 1, the biting rapid-fire stick shots of Drum Fill 2, and the sight and sound of his open hi-hat crashes beginning in Bar 21 of Drum Solo 2 are indeed some of the methods that became representative of Gene's style and sound.

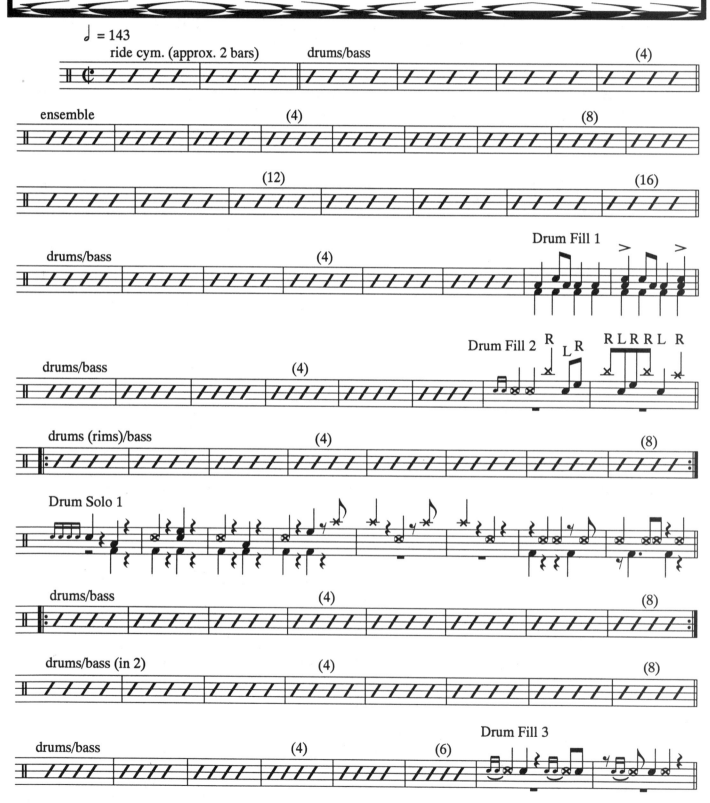

Sing, Sing, Sing (1937)

It had to have been the monstrously popular "Sing, Sing, Sing," Gene's signature piece, that prompted Rodgers & Hart, the great songwriting team of that era, to pen the following lyrics heard in their tune "I Like To Recognize The Tune" . . . "A man like Krupa plays the drums like thunder, but the melody lays six feet under." Certainly, a back-handed compliment of a sort but one that helps to point out the omnipresence of Gene's reputation at that time. His timekeeping on this version of the immortal "Sing . . ." is played almost entirely on the floor tom (hence the "thunder") with just a few snare/cymbal flourishes. On the other version of the tune (1971) on the video, he is seen employing snare/cymbal/bass timekeeping patterns during the ensemble sections.

71

Avalon

Bars 1-8 and 29-30 of the drum solo are totally devoted to a particular use of stick shots. The left stick, after it is struck by the right stick, plays a very light, *ghosted* if you will, press roll lasting just an instant and ending before the next stick shot is received from the right hand. This subtle, delicate, and enormously effective technique is one that Gene picked up from some of the popular players of the 1920s. Jim Chapin . . . "Gene heard that first from Baby Dodds (King Oliver's band) and Zutty Singleton (Louie Armstrong's band). They did that, but before them it was a vaudevillian thing and before that it might've been related to the old back stickings (a "sticks-hitting-together" technique) of drummers from the marching bands of the Civil War. All those tricks were around. They were just waiting to be applied to jazz" . . . and Gene was, of course, one of the first players to employ and develop the technique in that context.

Leave Us Leap

This video clip cuts right to the heart of what gave Gene the immense popularity he enjoyed by this time (1945) in his career. He was the showman king of swing music and, as his peers attest, it was the essential element from which his incredible reputation was forged. While his superlative and innovative playing led the way for the drummers of the '30s and '40s, his showmanship was regarded as the ingredient that truly connected him to the audience and hence to his being regarded by many as the most popular musician of all time. Jim Chapin . . . "Unless you were there you don't realize the impact (of his showmanship). He believed it! When he rehearsed it was the same way. The other guys would turn around during rehearsal and he'd be playing the same way as if it were a performance but there was nobody there but the players." It was the only way he knew how to play the drums . . . animated and marionette-like. This particular clip captures that quality within the confines of three blisteringly powerful short solos.

Cowbell Lick
(from "The Gene Krupa Story"/Sal Mineo segment)

This engaging pattern is employed in the video on "The Big Noise From Winnetka" (last two bars of Drum Solo 2), and with a slight variation (left hand on the snare instead of the bass drum) earlier in that song (Drum Fill 2). Here in the "The Gene Krupa Story" sequence, one gets a bit more insight into it as Gene teaches it to Sal Mineo. Jim Chapin . . . "That's a trick older than God. It was a New Orleans thing that was easier to do then because, don't forget they had those big bass drums (26")."

I'm A Ding-Dong Daddy From Dumas

This wonderful moment reunited the original Benny Goodman Band to the howls and delight of the audience. Here, in one of the last filmed documents of his playing (1972), Gene's exciting roll-off sets up the tune aptly. His solo is rich with the syncopated snare cracks and rim shots that were always so characteristic of his playing.

Sing, Sing, Sing (1971)

The close-camera shots and excellent audio quality in this video clip offer great access to what Gene is playing not just in his solo sections, but also in all the time-keeping sections. The viewer is here afforded great perspective to some of the ways Gene kept time and the tune was chosen to be transcribed from beginning to end (instead of just the solos) for this reason. Notice in the first three time-keeping sections (A, B, then A again) how Gene basically keeps time on the hi-hat alone with just the sparsest of kicks that he drops in on the bass drum. Louie Bellson, in the video, refers to this as "dropping bombs" and the effect of these is quite dramatic, rhythmically speaking, within the context of the tune. Throughout the vibes solo Gene extends the body of his time-keeping to include cross-sticks, snare and tom shots, and ruffs that he coordinates with more delightfully placed "bombs." The drum intro was transcribed with the stickings to give added insight into what was perhaps the most famous drum solo ever recorded and certainly the most well-known Krupa tune.

78

Drum Solo 3

ensemble

Drum Battle

The technical ability Gene exhibits here in the second of his two solos indicates clearly that he still had it very late in his career (1971). The 3 or 4 bars of explosive sixteenth notes that he plays at this point certainly catch the viewer/listener off guard AND one gets the feeling that the assembled battling drummers were also a bit surprised, pleasantly of course, to hear the old man blow like that.

Just A Riff (1947)

This clip shows just how much accents and rim shots were a part of the Krupa thing. Drum Solo 1 employs them in a triplet context while Drum Solo 2 has Gene using them within sixteenth note phrases that continue when the ensemble rejoins him. Also, the 16 bar section following Drum Solo 1 is noteworthy as it is the only other time in the entire video (besides the 1971 version of "Sing, Sing, Sing") that the camera affords one a good visual perspective of Gene's snare/bass/cymbal timekeeping styles.

Drum Solo 2

ensemble

Opus #145

The comedic element of this video clip evidently called for super, hand-to-hand chops just at that moment. It was a good excuse for Gene to show off his capabilities in that area. Nothing here but brilliantly executed, very up-tempo triplets on the snare with plenty of the rim shot accents that, again, were so much a part of his style.

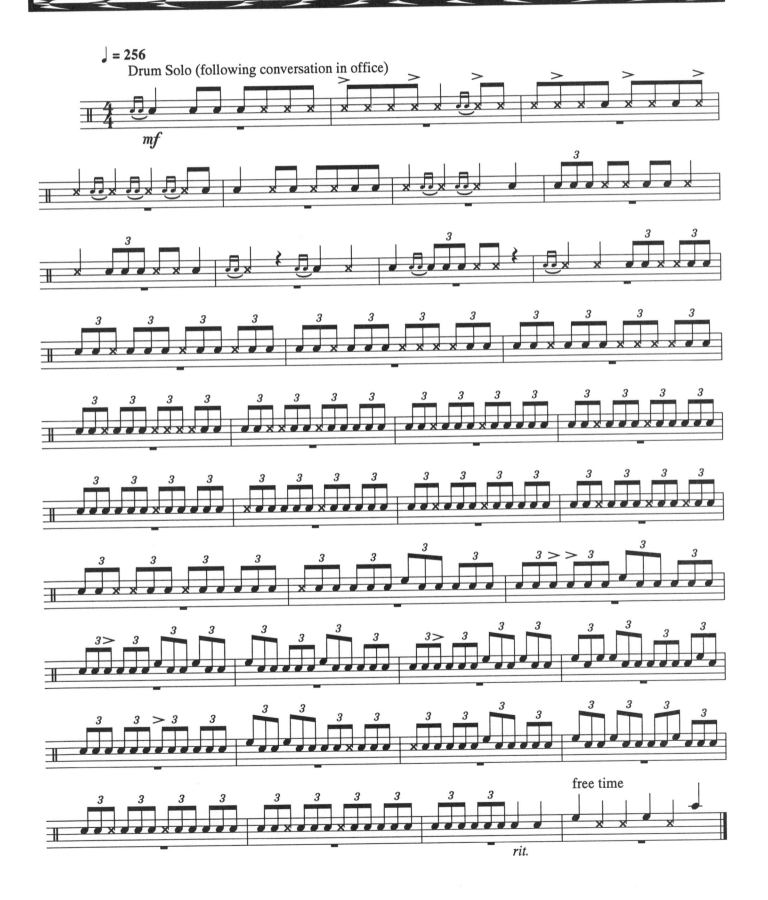

Caravan

Gene begins the tune with speedy paradiddles between the snare and cymbal and then goes onto the drums with a similar paradiddle oriented, yet undiscernible, sticking. As the piece begins, the moodiness of Caravan's haunting melody, as performed here by the ensemble, suggests the possibility of a somewhat experimental performance of the piece. Indeed, Drum Solo 1 is counterpointed by a stand-up bass, quarter note triplet motif which imposes a feeling of 3 within Gene's 4/4 soloing. At bar 21 of the solo, his eighth note triplet sticking changes in such a way that it appears he is going to switch over and join the bass player in the 3 feel. 16 bars later the total transition is made (the 3/4 feel is more easily expressed here as 6/8). Drum Solo 3 features a wonderful array of accented sixteenth note triplets within the new time signature. Also of note is the constant hi-hat pattern in all the 6/8 sections which has the left foot playing on 2, 4 and 6 throughout. All in all this video clip portrays a side of Gene somewhat different than most archival Krupa pieces present.

ensemble

Drum Solo 3

harmonica solo 3

36 BARS

time

4 BARS

harmonica solo 4

24 BARS

rit.

Up An Atom

Brute speed is of course the focus of both the Drum Fill and Drum Solo on this clip. Gene approaches each in the same way . . . with burning sixteenth notes on the snare drum, the phrases of which are formed by accents placed on the snare or on the tom. It's interesting to note that Drum Fill 2 of the Drum Battle clip (last sequence on the tape) has him calling upon the same technique and just as capably, despite the fact that it is 25 years later.